HAL LEONARD CHRISTMAS PIANO FOR KIDS

PIANO METHOD

12 Popular Christmas Solos for Beginners

ARRANGED BY JENNIFER LINN

T0071516

To access audio visit:
www.halleonard.com/mylibrary

Enter Code
3517-4898-5215-5344

ISBN 978-1-4950-9848-2

7777 W. BLUEMOUND RD. P.O. BOX 13819 MILWAUKEE, WI 53213

Visit Hal Leonard Online at
www.halleonard.com

INTRODUCTION

Even brand new beginners will be able to play these popular Christmas songs! *Christmas Piano For Kids* is a useful supplement to the *Piano For Kids Method Book*. Like the method book, the songs begin with the simplest pre-staff notation and progress to easy notation on the staff. The book includes access to audio tracks online for download or streaming, using the unique code inside this book!

–Jennifer Linn

ABOUT THE AUDIO

To access the accompanying audio, simply go to **www.halleonard.com/mylibrary** and enter the code found on page 1 of this book. This will grant you instant access to every file. You can download to your computer, tablet, or phone, or stream the audio live—and you can also use our *PLAYBACK+* multi-functional audio player to slow down or speed up the tempo, change keys, or set loop points. This feature is available exclusively from Hal Leonard and is included with the price of this book!

For technical support, please email support@halleonard.com

CONTENTS

Pre-Staff

On Staff

JOLLY OLD ST. NICHOLAS

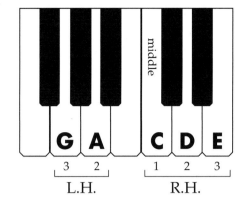

Traditional 19th Century American Carol

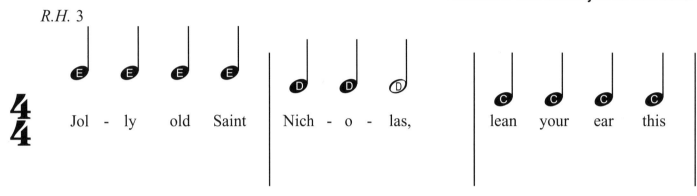

R.H. 3

Jol - ly old Saint | Nich - o - las, | lean your ear this

4 |

way! | Don't you tell a | sin - gle soul

L.H. 2

Teacher Duet (Student plays two octaves higher than written.)

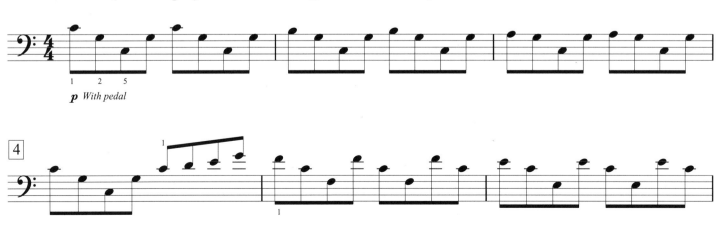

p With pedal

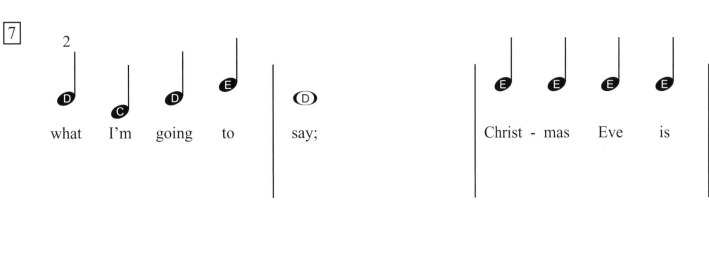

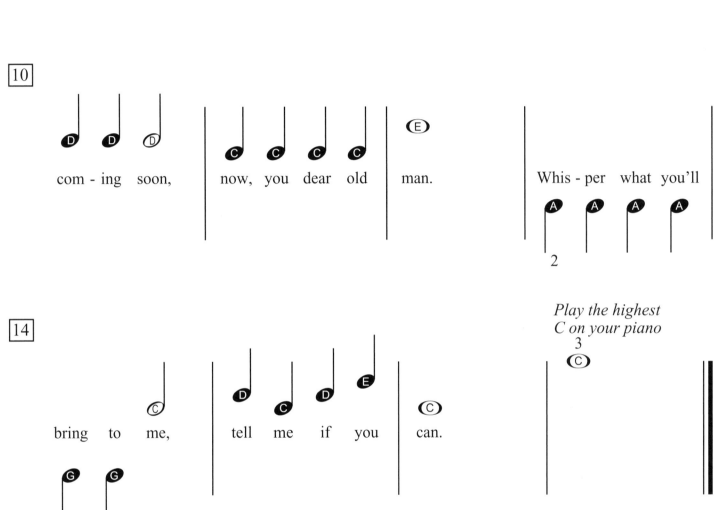

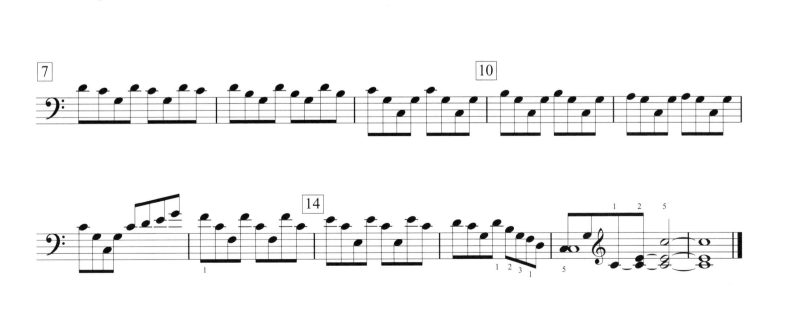

GO, TELL IT ON THE MOUNTAIN

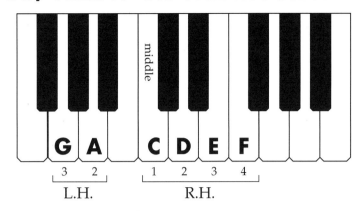

African-American Spiritual
Verses by John W. Work, Jr.

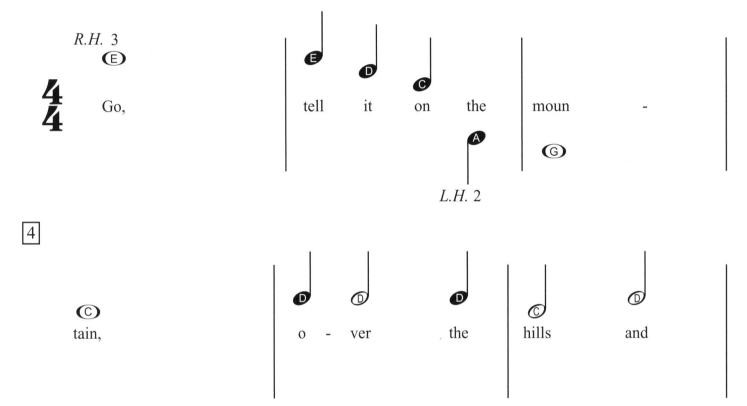

R.H. 3
Ⓔ Go,
tell it on the moun -
Ⓐ Ⓖ
L.H. 2

4
Ⓒ tain,
Ⓓ o - Ⓓ ver Ⓓ the Ⓒ hills Ⓓ and

Teacher Duet (Student plays one octave higher than written.)

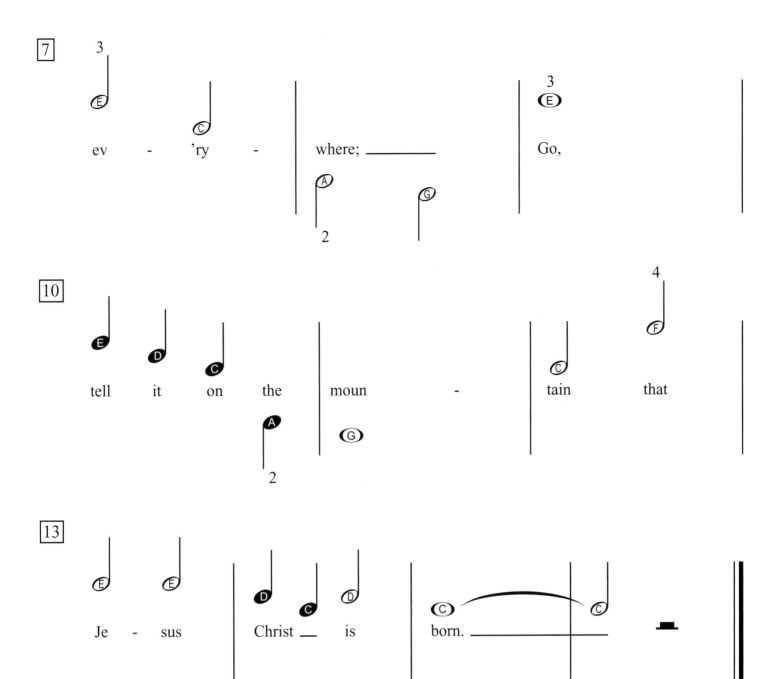

JINGLE BELLS

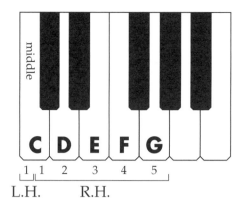

Words and Music by
J. Pierpont

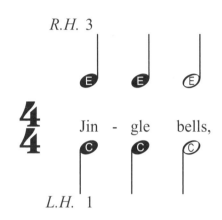

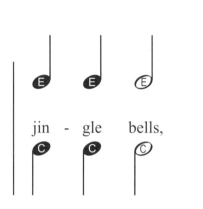

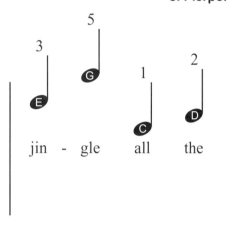

Jin - gle   bells,   jin - gle   bells,   jin - gle   all   the

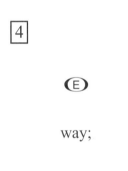

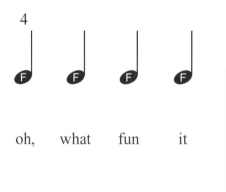

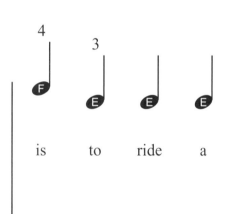

way;   oh,   what   fun   it   is   to   ride   a

Teacher Duet (Student plays as written.)

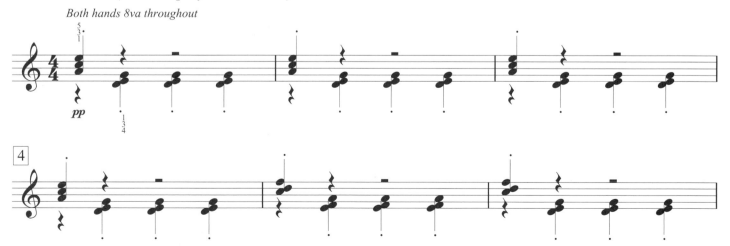

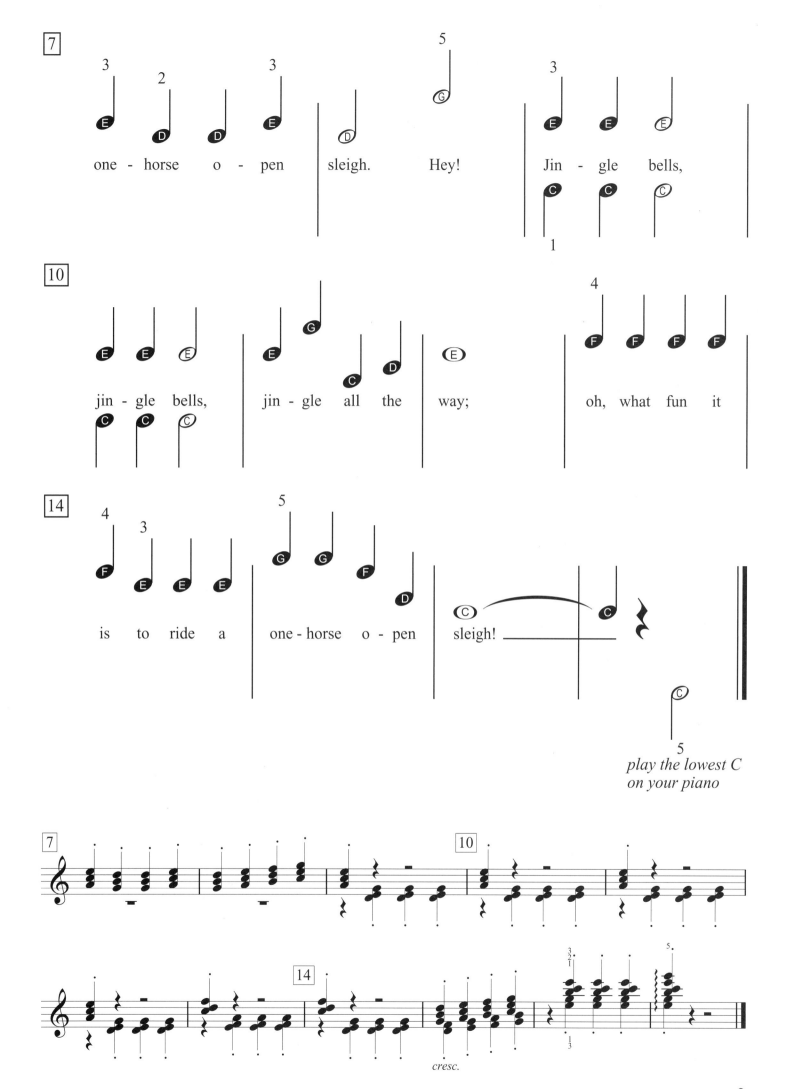

play the lowest C
on your piano

WE THREE KINGS OF ORIENT ARE

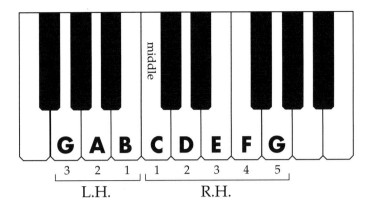

Words and Music by
John H. Hopkins, Jr.

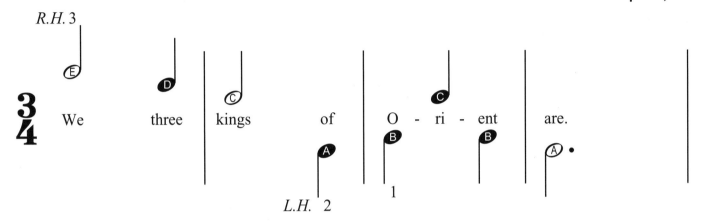

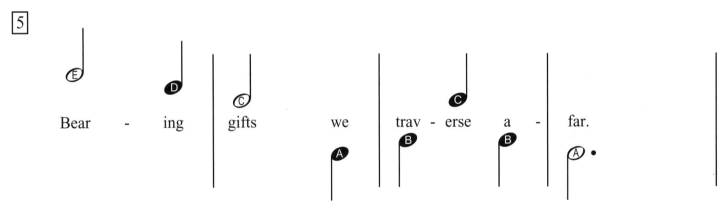

Teacher Duet (Student plays two octaves higher than written.)

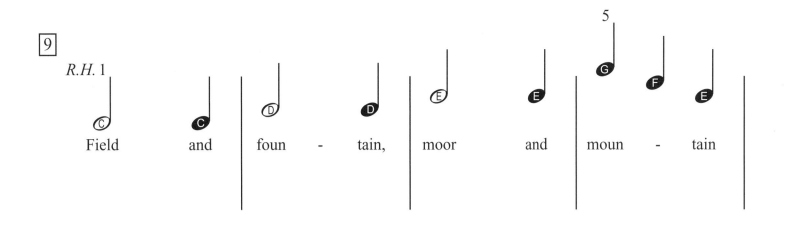

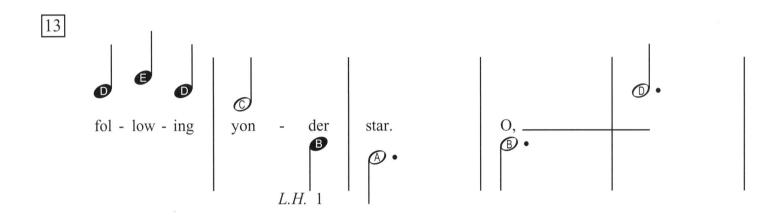

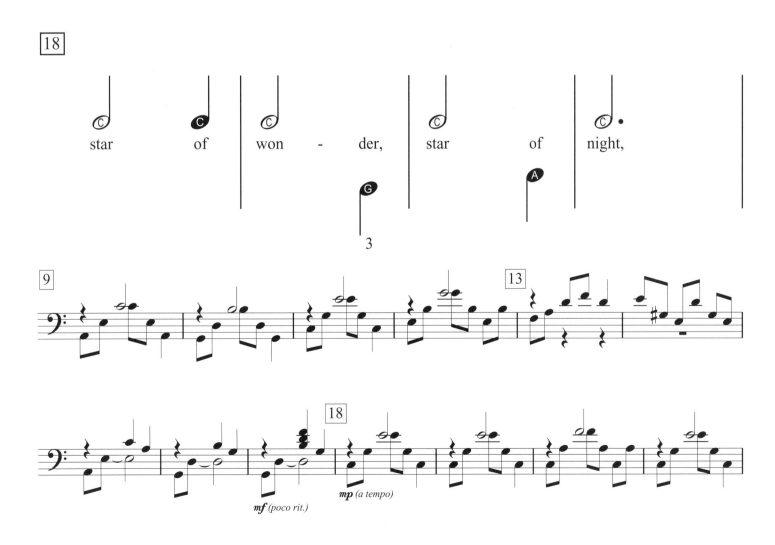

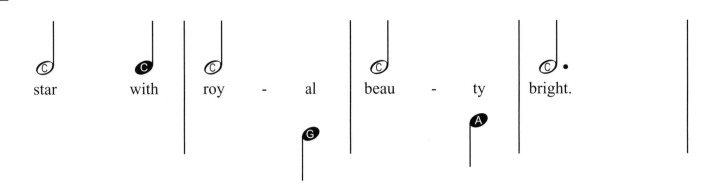

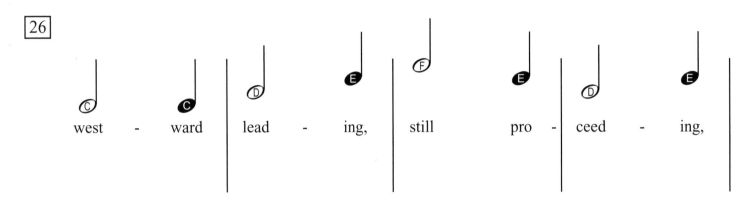

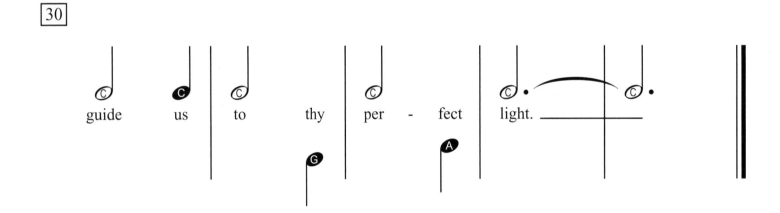

THE LITTLE DRUMMER BOY

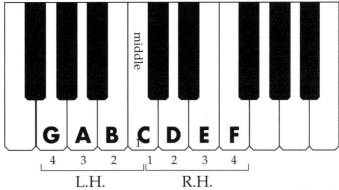

**Words and Music by Harry Simeone,
Henry Onorati and Katherine Davis**

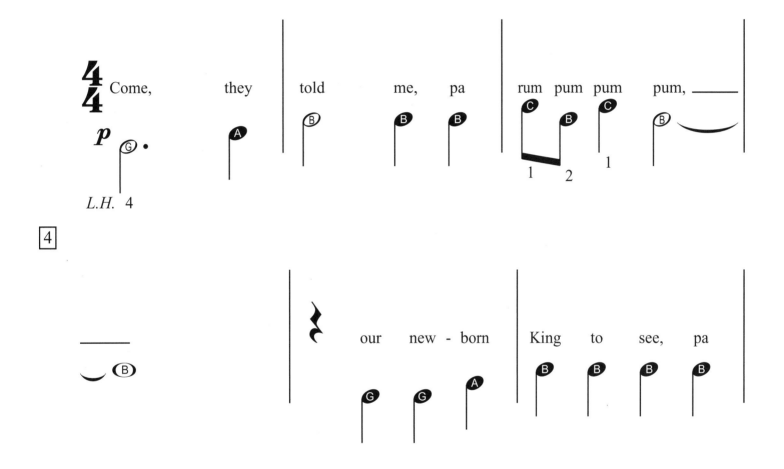

Teacher Duet (Student plays one octave higher than written.)

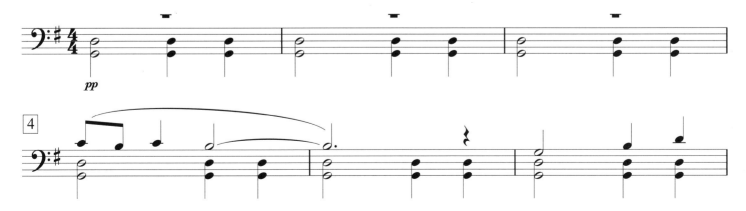

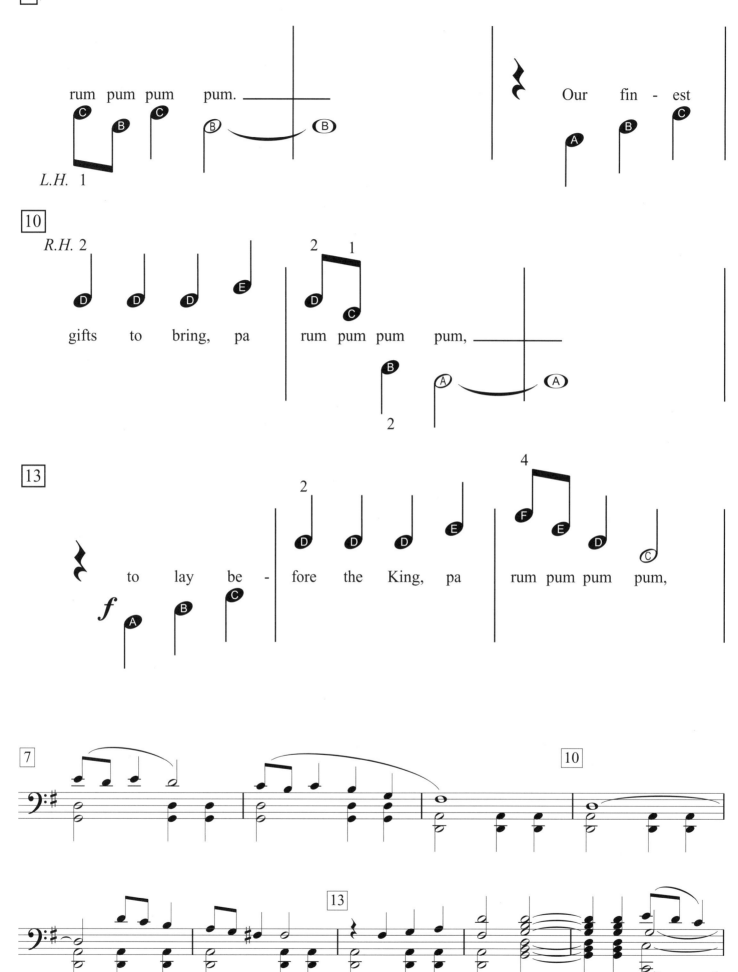

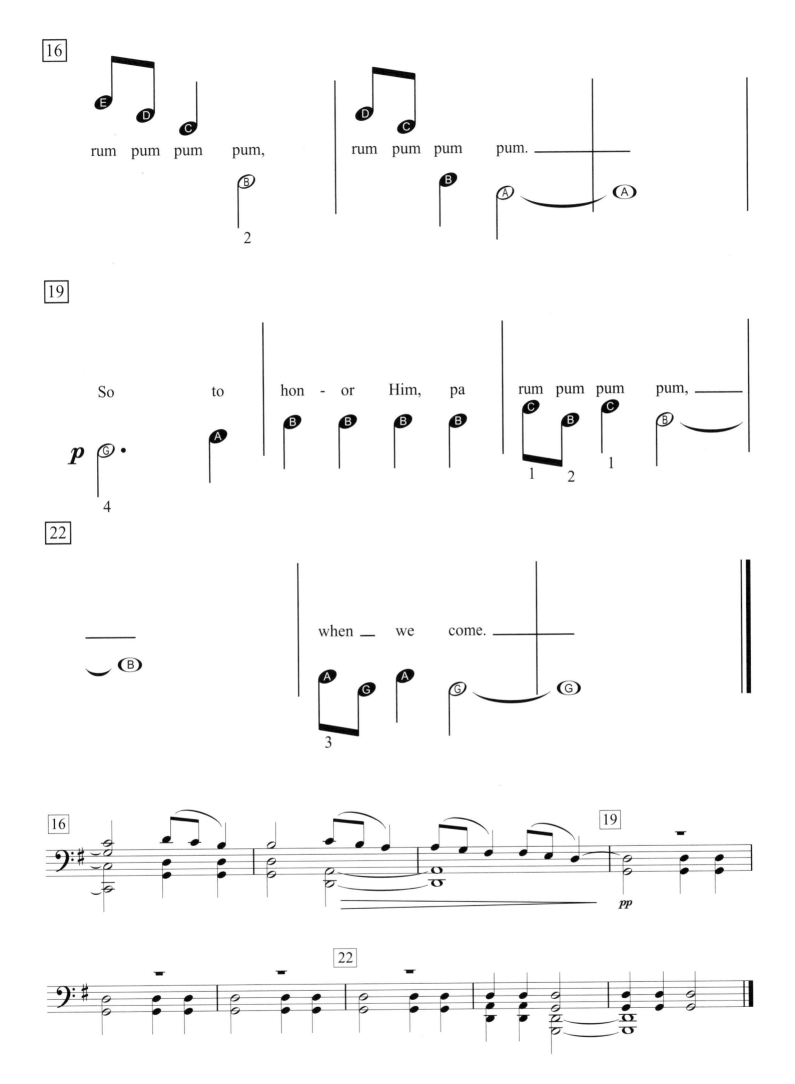

UP ON THE HOUSETOP

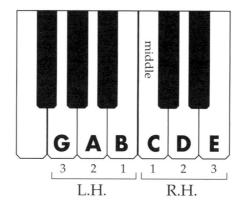

Words and Music by
B.R. Hanby

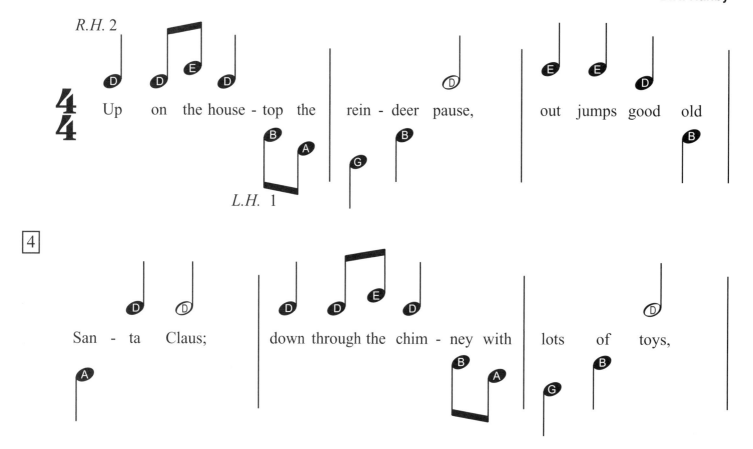

Teacher Duet (Student plays one octave higher than written.)

MARY, DID YOU KNOW?

HAND POSITION SHIFT

In this book, when you see a fingering in a shading triangle, your hand will need to move higher or lower on the keyboard depending on the direction of the triangle.

Words and Music by Mark Lowry and Buddy Greene

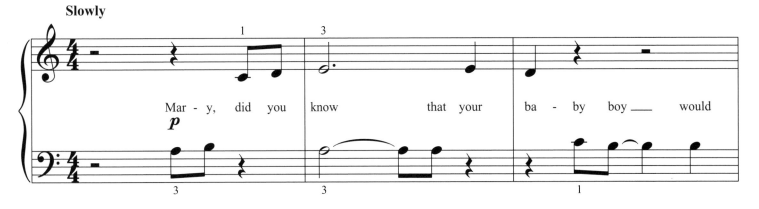

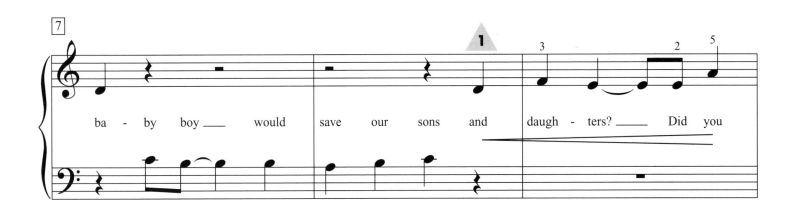

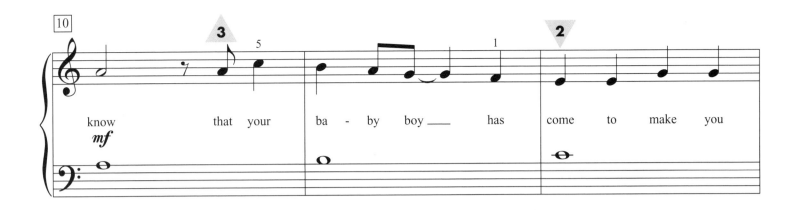

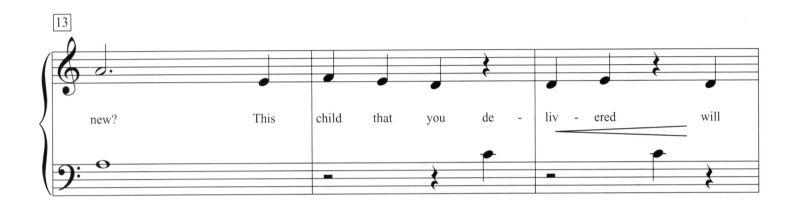

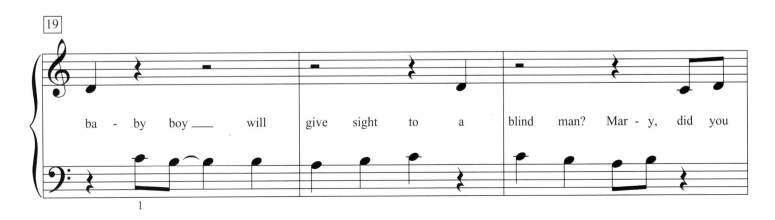

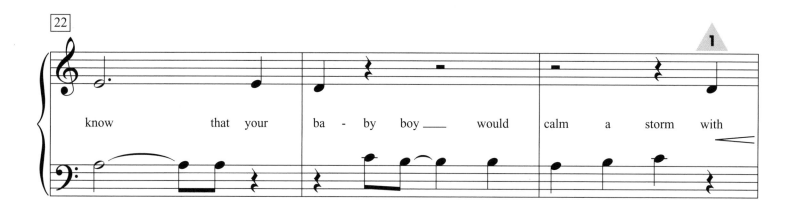

know that your ba - by boy   would calm a storm with

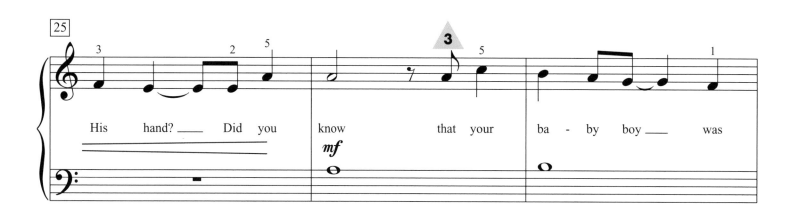

His hand?   Did you know that your ba - by boy   was

mf

heav - en's per - fect Lamb, and the sleep - ing Child you're

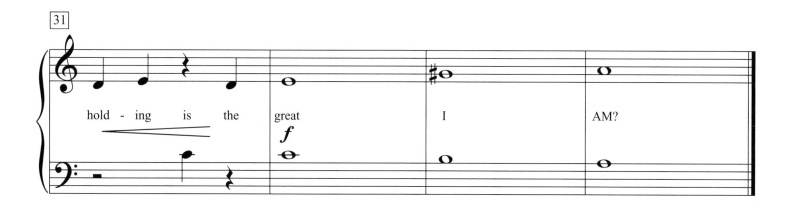

hold - ing is the great I AM?

f

RUDOLPH THE RED-NOSED REINDEER

Music and Lyrics by
Johnny Marks

Briskly

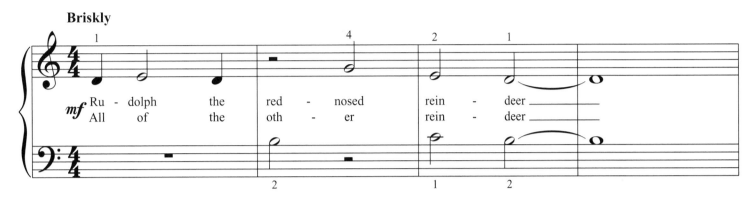

Ru - dolph the red - nosed rein - deer
All of the oth - er rein - deer

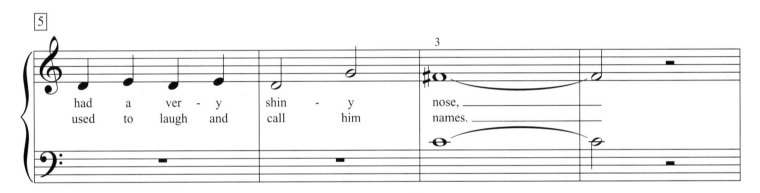

had a ver - y shin - y nose,
used to laugh and call him names.

and if you ev - er saw it,
They nev - er let poor Ru - dolph

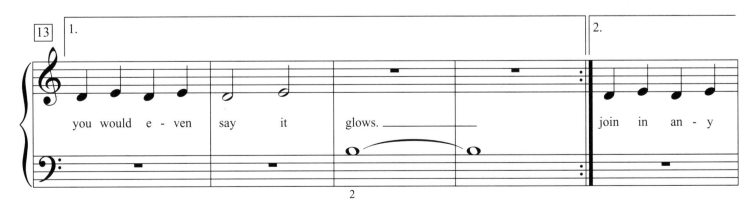

1. you would e - ven say it glows.   **2.** join in an - y

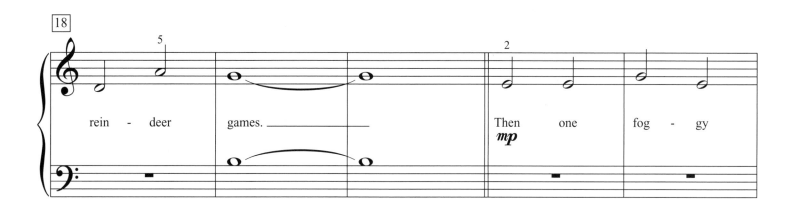

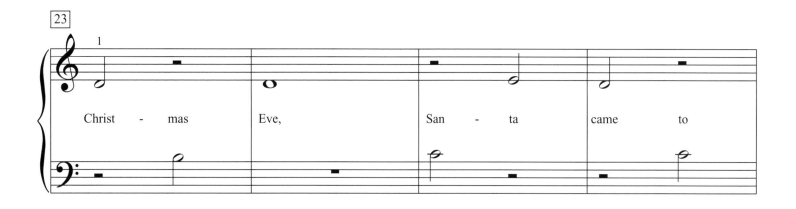

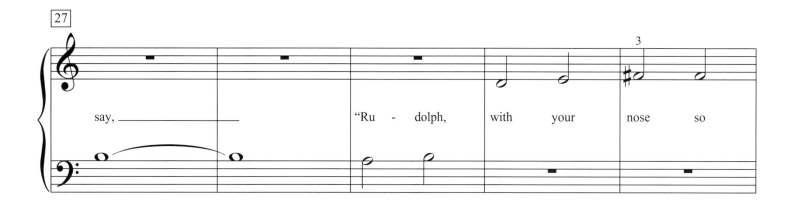

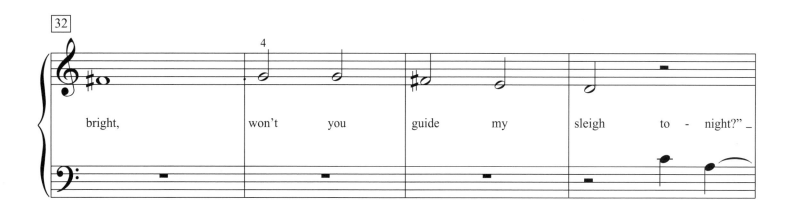

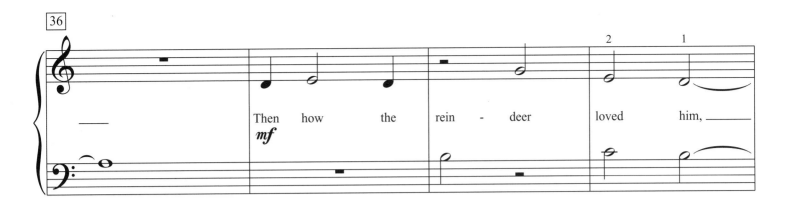

Then how the rein - deer loved him, *mf*

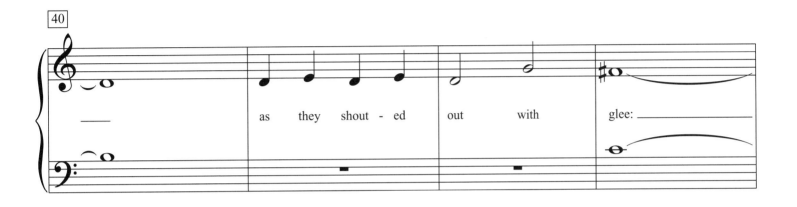

as they shout - ed out with glee:

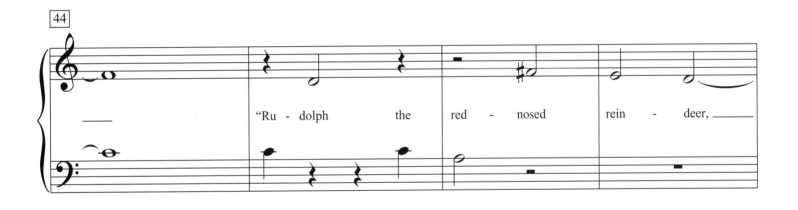

"Ru - dolph the red - nosed rein - deer,

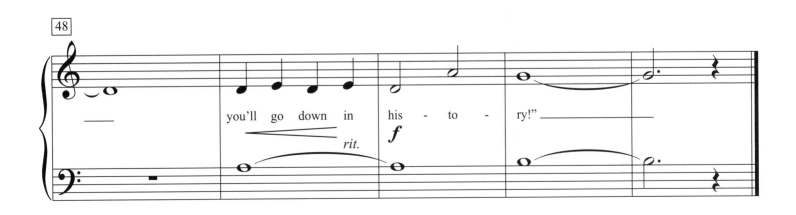

you'll go down in his - to - ry!" *rit.* *f*

SLEIGH RIDE

Music by Leroy Anderson

Joyfully

THE TWELVE DAYS OF CHRISTMAS

Traditional English Carol

Cheerfully fast

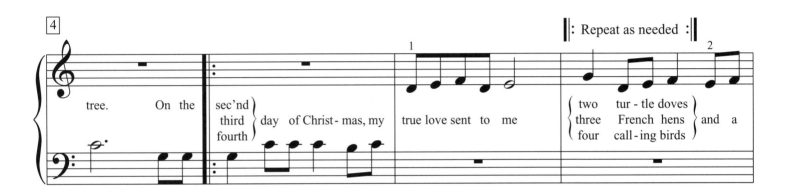

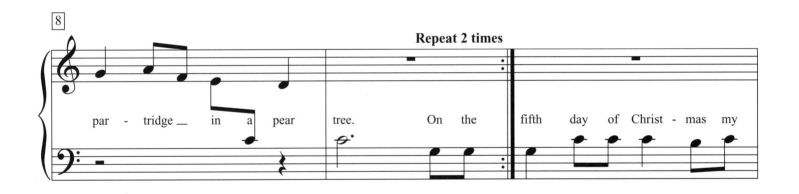

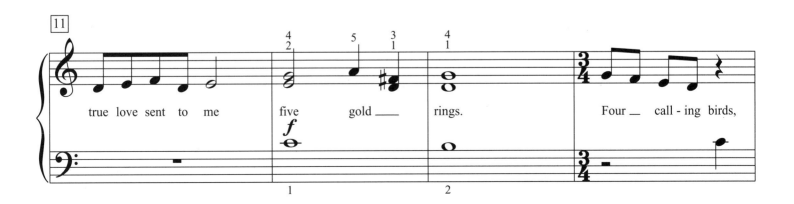

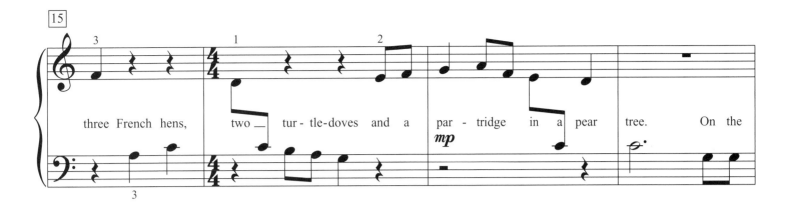

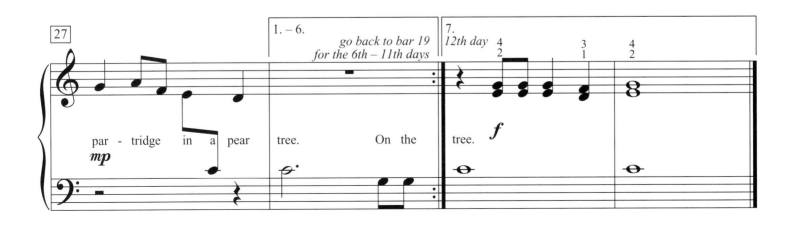

JINGLE BELL ROCK

Words and Music by Joe Beal
and Jim Boothe

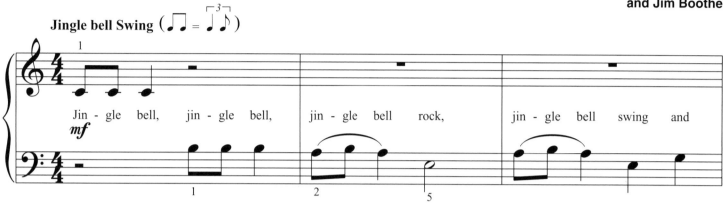

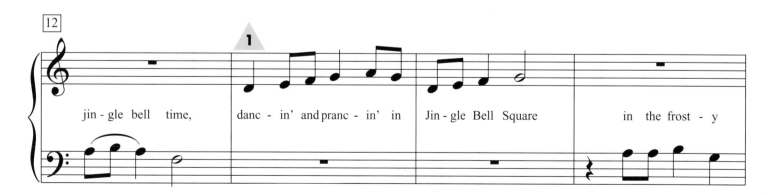

air. What a bright time, it's the right time, to rock the night a-

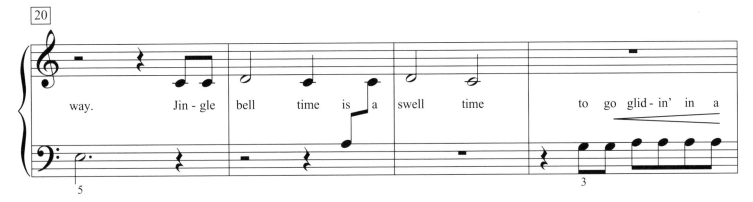

way. Jin-gle bell time is a swell time to go glid-in' in a

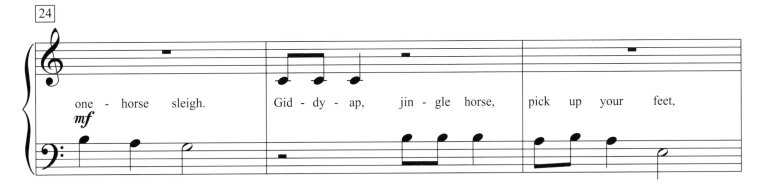

one-horse sleigh. Gid-dy-ap, jin-gle horse, pick up your feet,

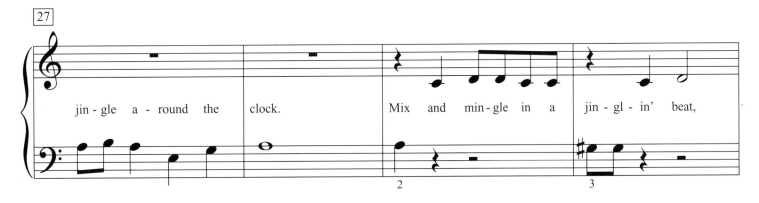

jin-gle a-round the clock. Mix and min-gle in a jin-gl-in' beat,

that's the jin-gle bell, that's the jin-gle bell, that's the jin-gle bell rock.

I WANT A HIPPOPOTAMUS FOR CHRISTMAS
(Hippo the Hero)

Words and Music by
John Rox

Brightly (♩♩ = ♪ ♪) swing eighths

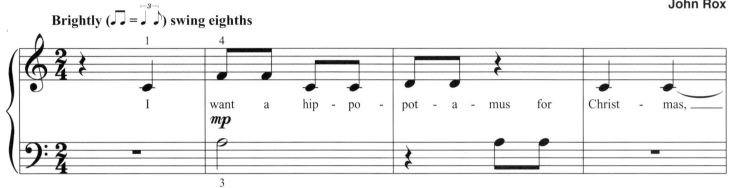

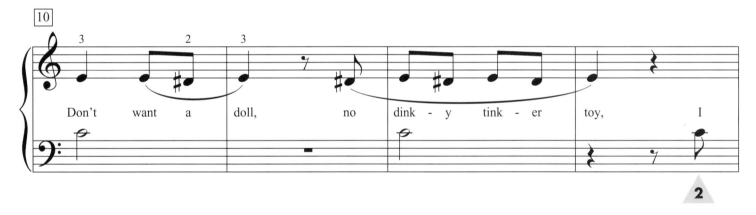

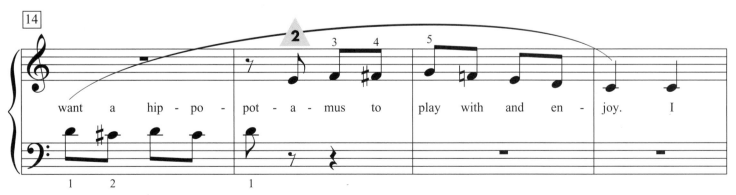

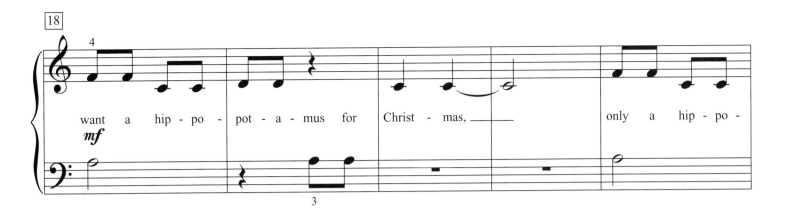

want a hip-po-pot-a-mus for Christ-mas, _____ only a hip-po-

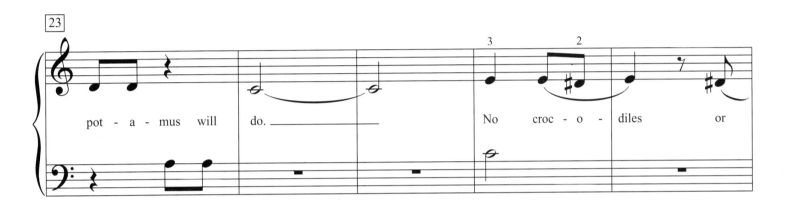

pot-a-mus will do. _____ No croc-o-diles or

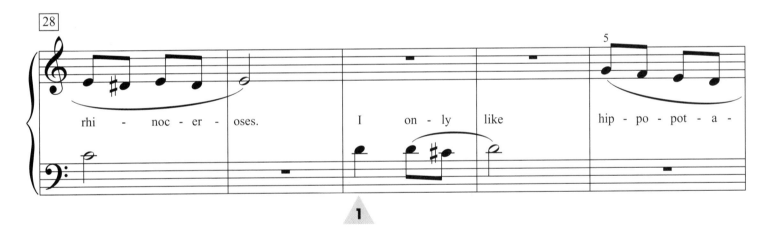

rhi-noc-er-oses. I on-ly like hip-po-pot-a-

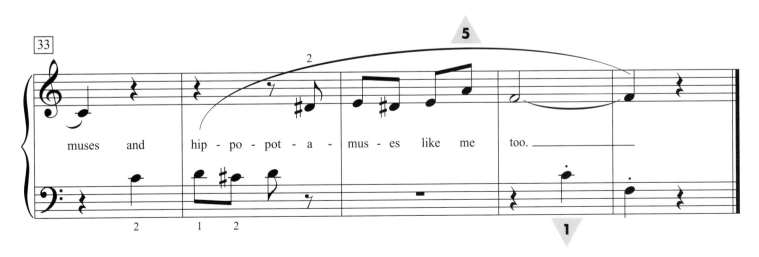

muses and hip-po-pot-a-mus-es like me too. _____

HAL LEONARD METHODS FOR KIDS

BASS FOR KIDS
by Chad Johnson

INCLUDES TAB

Bass for Kids is a fun, easy course that teaches children to play bass guitar faster than ever before. Popular songs such as "Crazy Train," "Every Breath You Take," "A Hard Day's Night" and "Wild Thing" keep kids motivated, and the clean, simple page layouts ensure their attention remains focused on one concept at a time. Lesson topics include selecting a bass, holding the bass, hand position, reading music notation and counting, and more. Audio examples are accessed online for download or streaming.

00696449 Book/Online Audio............................$12.99

GUITAR FOR KIDS
by Bob Morris and Jeff Schroedl

Popular songs such as "Yellow Submarine," "Hokey Pokey," "I'm a Believer," "Surfin' U.S.A.," "This Land Is Your Land" and "Hound Dog" in *Guitar for Kids* will keep students motivated. The method is equally suitable for students using electric or acoustic guitars. The accompanying online audio contains more than 30 tracks for demonstration and play-along and is accessed using the unique code printed inside each book. No tablature included.

00865003 Book/Online Audio............................$12.99

GUITAR FOR KIDS SONGBOOK

Guitar for Kids Songbook is a useful supplement to the *Guitar for Kids Method Book* as the songs follow the chords in the order they are taught, beginning with simple two- and three-chord songs and ending with songs that contain four and five chords. 10 songs, including: At the Hop • Don't Worry, Be Happy • Electric Avenue • Every Breath You Take • Feelin' Alright • Fly like an Eagle • Jambalaya (On the Bayou) • Love Me Do • Paperback Writer • Three Little Birds.

00697402 Book/Online Audio............................$9.99

GUITAR FOR KIDS METHOD & SONGBOOK
by Bob Morris and Jeff Schroedl

This convenient pack combines the *Guitar for Kids* Method and Songbook for all-in-one learning.

00697403 Book/Online Audio............................$19.99

HARMONICA FOR KIDS
by Eric Plahna

Harmonica for Kids is an accessible course that teaches children to play harmonica faster than ever before. The price of the book includes access to audio play-along and demonstration tracks online for download or streaming. Lessons include topics such as hand position, basic chord playing, learning melodies, and much more. Over 30 songs are featured in the book, including: All My Loving • Happy Birthday to You • Jingle Bells • Over the River and Through the Woods • Scarborough Fair • Take Me Out to the Ball Game • This Land Is Your Land • You Are My Sunshine • and more.

00131101 Book/Online Audio............................$12.99

PIANO FOR KIDS
by Jennifer Linn

Piano for Kids teaches children to play piano or keyboard quicker than ever before. Every new song builds on concepts they have learned in previous songs, so kids can progress with confidence. Popular songs such as "Let It Go," "Beauty and the Beast," "Over the Rainbow," "Heart and Soul," "We Will Rock You" and more famous classical/folk tunes will keep kids motivated. The clean, simple page layouts ensure their attention remains on each new concept.

00156774 Book/Online Audio............................$12.99

PIANO FOR KIDS: CHRISTMAS
by Jennifer Linn

A perfect companion to the *Piano for Kids* Hal Leonard Method instruction book, this Christmas songbook features a dozen yuletide favorites for developing pianists. Includes: Go, Tell It on the Mountain • I Want a Hippopotamus for Christmas • Jingle Bell Rock • Jingle Bells • Mary, Did You Know? • Rudolph the Red-Nosed Reindeer • Up on the Housetop • We Three Kings of Orient Are • and more. Includes access to online audio tracks for each song.

00238915 Book/Online Audio............................$12.99

UKULELE FOR KIDS
by Chad Johnson

Popular songs such as "Yellow Submarine," "The Hokey Pokey," "This Land Is Your Land," "Rock Around the Clock," "You Are My Sunshine" and "Barbara Ann" keep kids motivated, and the clean, simple page layouts ensure their attention remains focused on one concept at a time. The method can be used in combination with a teacher or parent. The accompanying online audio contains tracks for demonstration and play-along. Lessons include: selecting your uke; parts of the uke; holding the uke; hand position; reading music notation and counting; notes on the strings; C, F, C7, Am, G, B-flat, and Gm chords; strumming and picking; and more!

00696468 Book/Online Audio............................$12.99

UKULELE FOR KIDS SONGBOOK

Strum your favorite hits from Jason Mraz, Disney, U2 and more! This collection can be used on its own, as a supplement to the *Ukulele for Kids* method book or with any other beginning ukulele method. The songs are presented in order of difficulty using simple strumming notation – no music reading required. Demo tracks for each song are available for download online. Songs: Don't Worry, Be Happy • I'm Yours • The Lion Sleeps Tonight • Riptide • The Siamese Cat Song • and more.

00153137 Book/Online Audio............................$9.99

DRUMS FOR KIDS

This enjoyable course will teach children to play drumset faster than ever before. The method can be used in combination with a drum teacher or parent. Demonstration tracks are included online for download or streaming. Songs include: Another One Bites the Dust • Crazy Train • Free Fallin' • Living After Midnight • Old Time Rock & Roll • Stir It Up • When the Levee Breaks • and more.

00113420 Book/Online Audio............................$12.99

HAL•LEONARD®
www.halleonard.com

Prices, contents, and availability subject to change without notice.

0817